Shhhhhh . . . . Don't Tell

What is Hidden Will Become Known

Elizabeth Inman

Shhhhh . . . Don't Tell
What is Hidden Will Become Known
by Elizabeth Inman

Printed in the United States of America

ISBN 9781629522449

www.xulonpress.com

Table of Contents

Where you have been broken, others may be healed.
Where you have been betrayed,
others will receive love,
Where you have been misunderstood,
others will receive knowledge.
Where you have lost your way,
others will be delivered.

Sabrina L. Miller
August 2013

Chapter 1

The Blinding Light

Withhold not thou thy tender mercies from me,
O Lord: let thy loving-kindness and thy truth
continually preserve me. Psalm 40:11-17

Slowly I opened my eyes, and piercing light blinded
me, disorienting me. I blinked to make the light
go away, but it wouldn't. Scared and alone, I started
moving, and I heard them say, "She's coming out.";
then there was total darkness.

Time passed; what is time? Time is the indetermi-
nate, continued progress of being and existing in the
past, present and future, regarded as a whole. How
much time passed? My mind was racing; am I here
now, or is this the future? Am I reliving something from
my past, or is it just today? Confusion engulfed me,
and I slipped back into oblivion.

As I regained consciousness, I heard a rustling of
activity around me. I tried to move, but my body felt
like it weighed a million pounds. My arms were heavy;
I couldn't even move my fingers. "Try, try to move! I

have to get out of here; I have to do something now!" I couldn't move.

As I moaned and tried to make my body respond to my commands, I heard a female voice tell me it was okay. She told me I was doing fine. She said I was in recovery, and it was all over.

"What's all over? Where am I?" Then it hit me. I knew exactly where I was; I knew exactly what I had done. I wondered how they did it. Did they cut on me? I looked for pain, but had nothing physical I could detect. Then I felt it, a thick slow trickle. What was that? In that moment, I knew it was blood. I could feel it oozing out on the pad they had provided; I didn't know I would bleed.

A black cloud descended on me. As it hovered above me, and slowly made the trek into my soul, I knew that nothing ever again would be the same. What had I just done?

"For **innumerable evils have compassed me about and mine iniquities have taken hold of me, so I am not able to look up {SEE}** they are more than the hairs of my head; therefore my heart faileth me. Psalm 40:12

Chapter 2

You Are Not Supposed to Know

For nothing is secret, that shall not be made manifest; neither *any thing* hidden, that shall not be known and come abroad. Luke 8:17

Shhhhhh . . . . don't tell. Until I had my abortion, I did not know of one other girl who had ever killed her baby. In this day and age of "everything goes", there are still some skeletons in the closet that don't come out. Even though the secrecy of abortion is a lie from the pit of hell, it's just not something we can talk about. "For there is nothing hidden that will not be disclosed, and nothing concealed that will not be known or brought out into the open" (Luke 8:17). The events leading up to my abortion allowed me to find one girl who had aborted her baby, and she is the one who led me to my abortion. I wasn't actively seeking her; she was just there in my life. I did not know that just a few months before, she, too, had an abortion. It would be over twenty years later before I would come face-to-face with anyone who would admit to having an abortion.

Oh it is done; millions every year are committed, but it is NOT talked about or discussed. We just don't tell.

The shroud of secrecy covering this act is well protected. It's not even that society keeps it hidden; society accepts abortion. Laws are easily passed without much opposition, allowing us to kill our babies. Statistics are passed around like candy. Everyone knows everyone does it, but no one will talk about having it done. Even the girl who took me to mine never discussed her abortion with me, other than to say she had one. Today, in my 50s, I have yet to hear one testimony in person from a woman who has had an abortion, or from one who was going to abort and did not.

At this writing, I found statistics that one in three ladies abort a baby; another statistic has it as four in ten. The next time you are in a public place with a lot of people, take a look at them. Abortion affects men and women alike; abortion's stronghold has no gender. Those numbers are staggering, yet it is not talked about: It is kept hidden.

Society does not hide it; the ladies who have the abortions hide it. The shame and guilt that surround, invade and dominate these women get a grip on them that won't allow them to speak up for help and healing; they can't even cry out for hope. Even the men who fathered these babies won't talk about abortion. Women who have aborted take their daughters to have abortions.

There are a staggering number of ladies who aborted their babies that live in deception about what they did. They believe they are okay, that it didn't matter they aborted a baby, that there is nothing wrong with them and there are no after affects of having an abortion. Many of them believe the lie that there was no baby in their womb. Many are driven to performance and success. Others hide their memories while caring for their family, while some drown in sorrow and depression, never equating it to their actions from killing their baby.

I did a combination of all of the above for a very, very long time. I set out on a career in government, and nothing could stop me from reaching the top. When I did start a family after my abortion, nothing was going to stop me from being the epitome of the "perfect" mom. It was as if I could make up for my past mistakes by never making another mistake. What a lie!!!! If you had seen my life, you never would have guessed I had ever aborted, or that I ever suffered any ill effects from it. Inside, the drive I attributed to my "natural ambition to succeed" was really my way of anesthetizing the pain I held inside because I had killed my baby.

It was especially hard after my first baby was born. The depression I experienced was passed off as post-partum depression. Perhaps it was in part, but there is not a doubt in my mind I was reeling from the love of that newborn baby boy I had just given birth to, knowing I had killed one just like it a few years earlier.

Women abort babies because they believe there is no other way out. Whether it's their shame, the fear of shaming their families, financial need, overload, the stigma of pregnancy or fear, the result is the same, exasperation and isolation. No two stories are alike. This is my story, and it's not like any one else's story; yet, it's also familiar. Every time I talk with a woman who has had an abortion, I can see me somewhere in the story. You may be reading this and crying, not even knowing why you are crying.

Abortion also impacts the people around them. Often, someone other than the woman having the abortion pays for it, and they are impacted: Mothers and grandmothers are impacted: The father of the baby is impacted; it's often simply not real to him. After all, it's her body, not his. He is disconnected and does not know how to handle her emotions, or his own. He often won't even allow emotions to surface. He often feels he doesn't have a say about what the woman may do. Others voice their demand for the woman not to have that child. Everyone connected with a woman who has aborted suffers along with her, all in varying degrees and in varying ways.

The very word abortion offends people, and for very different reasons. If you are reading this book, and you've had an abortion, and you have suppressed all feelings and emotions about the abortion, this book may anger you. You may have started crying with the first chapter and can't stop. This verse has comforted me so many times and will comfort you now:

Who comforts us in all our tribulation, that we may be able to comfort them, which are in trouble, by the comfort therewith we ourselves are comforted by God. 2 Corinthians 1:4

Chapter 3

Getting to This Place

Be pleased, O Lord, to deliver me; O Lord, make haste to help me. Psalm 40:13

L oving parents raised me; they worked hard and did all they knew to be the best parents to my brothers, sister and I, and they succeeded. My parents were very young when they married, and very young when they started a family. By the time my dad was twenty-three and my mom was nineteen, they had four children under the age of four, with two of those twins. I can't even imagine the load of responsibility they faced day by day. As if four children that age weren't enough, the twins had colic for the first year, and the sound of crying babies seemed to never stop.

I often say they were babies raising babies, especially my mom. For some reason, there was a shroud of mystery about certain things. I didn't find out my mom had miscarried a baby after I was born until I was in my twenties. There are just some things you don't talk about.

As kids, we were in church more than not. I probably answered every altar call ever given at every vacation

Bible school and church summer camp I ever attended, and I attended a lot of them. I had my "not going to hell" exchange with God very early. I knew God loved me, especially when I was a "good girl"; I truly, truly loved Him.

There is no doubt in my mind God called me very early and very young in my life. I also desperately tried to erase and run from the molestation I was experiencing from a man who knew better than to mess with a small child. That experience planted seeds of doubt and insecurities in my heart that played a major role in my decision to abort many years later.

For many reasons I had myself convinced I could not talk to my parents about my active sex life after it started. Because of many lies in the world about teenage sex during that time, I believed many deceptions, and in my mind, I truly believed I could not talk to my parents. I fell in love at a very tender age, and was way too young to lose my virginity to the man of my youthful dreams. He and I attended church together, and were baptized at nearly the same time.

When my mom found out we were "messing around" (of course I never told her we went all the way), she did as any good parent of such a young girl would do; she forbid me to ever see him again. Her imposed separation eventually undid our relationship, and it ended. I was hurt beyond words and totally brokenhearted; he betrayed me, and allowed the imposed separation to end our love. I was so resentful to my mother for doing her job and keeping us apart. I held on to that resentment far into adulthood; and the stage was set that I could never discuss my sexual activity with my mom. Mom gave me the mother-daughter talk, and did her best to educate me. I could discuss the topic of sex with my mom, just not my sexual activity.

Unfortunately, a fire had been lit within me, and generational curses had set tracks on my life that urged me on to look for love in all the wrong places. I had been boy crazy all my life, and I was on a quest to find true, lasting love. I had never allowed God's love to fill me completely, and I was searching for a cheap replacement.

The enemy of lies and deceit of this world are strong, and they come to kill us and destroy us. "The thief cometh not, but for to steal, and to kill, and to destroy: I am come that they might have life, and that they might have it more abundantly," (John 10:10). I bought into the lie my mom would never understand. I bought into the lie I could handle things all by myself, that I knew more than anyone else. I bought into the lie that a man would love me more if I gave my precious gift to him.

Just out of high school, attending college in the very first semester, with all hope and promise surrounding me, I find out I am pregnant. The young man had just broken up with me because I made good grades and was going to college. He told me I was too good for him, and he would do nothing but mess up my future. At the time, he worked for the city as a garbage truck driver. He felt he did not add up to my expectations. Oh, he said he still loved me; he just couldn't match up to my big dreams of college and future. I thought I loved him. Once again, I was brokenhearted and abandoned: Now I am pregnant, and I don't know what to do. I am absolutely terrified and alone.

We had been broken up for just a few weeks when I called him and gave him the news. He said I was not his only girlfriend to get pregnant, and he would just do what he did last time; he would pay for the abortion. He never said he loved me: he never said he was sorry;

he never offered an alternative. He just brought me the money. That was the last time I ever heard from him.

Being a social butterfly, I had dozens of friends. I also was a leader among my friends, and what they thought of me mattered. I was the one they came to with their problems; I certainly was not supposed to have the problems. Once again, I bought into the lie of isolation, and I blocked myself off from everyone. I did not think I could live with the stigma of pregnancy outside of marriage; I could not shame my parents that way. I could not figure any way out.

> Let them be ashamed and confounded together that seeks after my soul to destroy it; let them be driven backward and put to shame that wish me evil. Let them be desolate for a reward of their shame that say unto me, "Aha aha".
> Psalm 40:14-15

Chapter 4

Not Everything
is Out of the Closet

Ye are of *your* father the devil, and the lusts
of your father ye will do. He was a murderer
from the beginning, and abode not in the truth,
because there is no truth in him. When he speaketh a lie, he speaketh of his own: for he is a liar,
and the father of it. John 8:44

In today's society, it's the cool thing to do to experi-
ment in bisexual behavior. No more is there a taint
on your reputation if you aren't a virgin. In fact, there is
a taint on your reputation if you are not sexually active;
and it's gone to the next level, girls experimenting
with girls.

Things were even different twenty years ago when I
was raising my sons. I was absolutely astounded when
I overhead my son at age eight discussing, on the way
home from Cub Scout camp, sexual things to do to a
girl. Being the good mother I wanted to be, and determined my children would ALWAYS be able to discuss
sex, even THEIR sex, with me, I set out to have the first

talk about the birds and the bees with my son. Never in a million years would I ever think his very first question at age eight would be the topic of oral sex. Oh my, even then things were progressing at a rapid age. Today, sex education is being taught as early as kindergarten!

Today, kids are exposed to sex at younger and younger ages. Sex is all over television; sex sells, and it's a part of a large portion of all advertising. I won't even get into the Internet and all the pornography available at the click of a mouse. If you are old enough to turn on a computer, you are exposed to sex.

It's no longer taboo to talk about sex: It's no longer taboo to talk about sex between the same genders. Kids at younger and younger ages are not just declaring their homosexuality, they are also asking for gender change operations. It's in the news, it's on the airwaves and it's all around us.

We really live in a society where anything goes. We really don't even talk about "coming out of the closet" as homosexual today like they did ten and twenty years ago. In fact, is there really a closet any-more in this society where everything is permissible? Homosexuality is almost revered in many circles. Laws are being passed daily, allowing open homosexual activity and same-sex marriages. In the same sense, sexual abuse is a topic discussed frequently on televi-sion. Men and women are openly talking of the abuse they suffered at the hands of another; that's because it IS all out of the closet. Or is it?

In a society where it seems everything goes, and truly it does, there are still secrets. What is a secret? Anything kept hidden from view, conducted in private and is not discussed openly is a secret. With laws in place for decades allowing abortion, why is it abortion is not discussed? In a society with so many laws in place openly supporting abortion, the ladies who abort still do not feel the freedom within them to openly discuss their abortion.

The shroud of secrecy a woman arrays herself in concerning her abortion keeps her hidden from view, out of the limelight. After all, our society has made abortion all about the woman, never the baby. Abortion is a woman's right to choose, not a baby's right to survive. Society says a baby is not a baby until it is born.

Recently, I posted a video on social media showing conception through birth. I was later verbally attacked by a man (of all things), explaining to me a baby is not a baby until birth, and a woman has a right to make whatever choice she so desires; this with no regard to human life since an embryo, of course, is not human life and videos, like the one I posted, were uncomfortable to women.

When the decision for this book was made, I shared my thoughts with a few of my closest loved ones. The very first time I shared, one of the precious ladies started crying almost as soon as I started talking. Until this moment, she did not have any idea I had aborted a baby. As I softly spoke, I made an assumption that as hard as she was sobbing that perhaps she, too, had aborted at some point in her life. When an opening in the conversation occurred, she confessed she had paid for a daughter's abortion and a granddaughter's abortion. She was in her late sixties, and had never ever confessed to anyone what she had done. She told me she has lived in torment with her secret all these years.

All of the deceit surrounding abortion makes it impossible to know how someone will respond to a conversation about abortion. If you have justified an abortion for many years, the last thing you want to hear is how life begins at conception. How can I tell my daughter not to abort when I did? If I've never talked about my abortion, how can I help my daughter to speak about her decision?

So many believers make one sin worse than another sin. It's OK to cheat on your wife, but it's not OK to say a racial slur: It's OK to abort a baby, but it's not OK to talk about it. Many women cannot imagine how their church family will accept or reject them if they knew they've had an abortion, or, worse, that they were pregnant out of wedlock with another man's baby that isn't their husband or many other unpardonable reasons. The fear of rejection is so strong! The belief they have no other way out is predominant.

What is it about abortion that makes it such a secret? Perhaps deep inside the woman, even though the lies represent that there is no baby inside of her womb, she just *knows* that yes, there was a real, live baby. Every child is a part of a mother: Every mother is a part of a child. There are even women who can hide their actions deep inside so far they live as though they never did have an abortion until the realization comes to surface and creates major problems later on in life.

> There is neither Jew nor Greek, there is neither bond nor free, there is neither male nor female: for ye are all one in Christ Jesus. Galatians 3:28

God tells us He sent Jesus so we all could be ONE. A teeny, tiny baby, upon conception, already is a spiritual being with a soul. The umbilical cord connects that baby to the mother and to God. They are ONE.

> And now I am no more in the world, but these are in the world, and I come to thee. Holy Father, keep through thine own name those whom thou

hast given me, that they may be one, as we *are one*. John 17:11

It's not out of the closet: It is hidden to the world that an embryo is truly a baby; a living, feeling life that has a soul and a spirit, and can experience love and pain. It's too easy to call it an *embryo*. After all, how many of you have ever really seen an embryo? Can you describe one? Do you know what a baby at ten weeks after conception looks like? How does she move, how does she thrive, how does she hear, how does she communicate, how does she bond with the mother at this tender age? No, if we call it an embryo or an egg, or better yet, if we just don't refer to "it" at all, then we never have to acknowledge the impact of abortion on the **baby.** After all, it's about the woman, right? **LIES!!!!!**

One of the biggest tools of the enemy is isolation. If he can isolate us, he believes he can destroy us. The enemy lies and tells us no one else will understand; no one else has ever felt what you are feeling; no one else has ever gone through this; no one else will ever forgive you, and the lies go on. As the woman believes the lies of the enemy, she further isolates herself. She never finds that safe person she can confess to and her healing is denied.

All the days wherein the plague *shall be* in him he shall be defiled; he *is* unclean: he shall dwell alone; without the camp *shall* his habitation *be*. Leviticus 13:46

Chapter 5

Here I Am

If you say, "see we did not know this," does He not consider it who weighs the heart? And does He not know it who keeps your soul and will He not render to man according to His work? Proverbs 24:12

So here I am, eighteen and alone, being driven to the clinic by virtual strangers. The drive from my hometown to the city where a clinic was available to perform the procedure was the longest drive of my life. To be totally truthful, I do not remember making the drive. I remember it was long; I cannot remember a single word spoken. I remember I was scared. I had never felt more alone, even though my friend and her mother were with me.

We parked the car and I walked up to the building. I remember red bricks on the building; in fact they were orange-red bricks, and there were a lot of them. I do not remember the address; I do not remember the route we took to get there once we were in the city. I do not remember the doctor's name or any of the nurses. Memory is a funny thing: Our mind has a way of blocking out those things that are just too painful to recall.

My friend and her mother dropped me off. I always believed it was because they were ashamed to be seen with me. Now I believe the pain of my friend's abortion was still too fresh on their minds. It was only the year before that my friend made this same journey to this same clinic, and her mother drove her there, just as they drove me here.

I walked up concrete stairs; I opened a door. All I can remember of the reception area is a faint mint green color; I think it's the color of the walls. I remember a lamp emitting a muffled yellow ray of light into the room. I don't remember how that room smelled, but I remember feeling cold, very, very cold.

Here I am. They call my name, and it begins. They take me into a tiny room; I fill out paperwork. I used my real name, even though I argued that point with myself. I answered the questions as honestly as I could. They asked if I had ever used birth control; I was ashamed to say no. You see, I had gone to a doctor for birth control just two months prior. All alone, I endured my first pelvic exam. I *knew* I desperately needed birth control, but I was too afraid to follow through. I was absolutely petrified my mom would find out. When I say I was convinced I could not talk to my mom, I really believed it. Today, I recognize that was a lie I accepted as truth.

I guess if I had to use a word to describe how I was feeling sitting in this little intake room, I would say numb; not numb enough to not feel fear, to feel alone, to tremble and to doubt. I had no idea if I was making a good decision; I had counseled with no one. I had no idea if this would hurt. I had no idea if I would be scarred physically, and I certainly had no idea how I would be scarred emotionally and spiritually. I did know

I had a baby inside of me. So when the admittance clerk asked if I had any questions, I wanted to know if it would hurt the baby. I wanted to know how big my baby was. Little did I know how big the plot to deceive was, and how it *would unfold.*

She asked me if I had ever been around chickens and hens on a farm. I told her I grew up on a farm, and we raised chickens. She said the *"embryo"* (emphasis added) was no different than a chicken egg. She asked if I had ever cracked open a chicken egg and seen the little white sperm attached to the yellow yoke. When I said yes, she explained that was exactly what the *"embryo"* looked like, and there was no life there; there was no movement and there was nothing that would resemble a baby at all. As best as I can recall, I estimate I was approximately ten weeks pregnant at this time.

As naïve as it sounds, that was the exact answer I needed. For me, I had to be able to detach from any concept or perception of a "baby" inside of me. From that moment on, it was an *"embryo"* that had no life, and all I was doing was throwing away a bad egg.

At ten weeks, the baby is no longer an embryo, but is actually a fetus. The baby's tissues and organs are rapidly developing at this point. Uncontrolled movements and twitches occur as muscles, the brain and nerve pathways begin to develop. The baby's head is still bigger than the rest of the body at ten weeks. The brain is developing at a rapid rate, and the nervous system is actually responsive, with many internal organs starting to function. The gender is already established. Though I will never know for sure, I am convinced I carried a precious little girl.

At ten weeks (like the picture on the front cover of this book of a ten week old fetus in the mother's womb), there is no doubt that that it is a baby. The heartbeat is almost fully developed at this point. Inside the baby's mouth are all the tooth buds that will eventually burst through her gums once she's six months old or so. There are also taste buds on her tongue. She has a functioning digestive tract capable of moving food all the way to her bowels. Within the week, this baby will be able to yawn, swallow, close her eyelids, and will be spending her days sucking, wrinkling her forehead and turning her head as she moves around her mother's uterus; approximately the size of a plum, and already has a sense of smell. Downy hair has started on the baby's skin, and true identity markings are in place, making them a unique individual. There is nothing at this point (or any point since conception) that resembles a chicken's egg.

A stranger led me to that room, a stranger put me under; I was invaded by a stranger. My baby died at the hand of a stranger and her mother (I will always believe my baby was a girl). I woke during the procedure to hear the voices of strangers, and I came to in recovery in the presence of strangers.

I was actually driven home by strangers, even though the girl was my friend, and I had spent the night in her home on several occasions and knew of her mother; on this day, I was among strangers. Nothing seemed right, nothing felt right, nothing was right and nothing would ever be right again for a very long time.

Here I am, changed.

And the revolters are profound to make slaughter, though I *have been* a rebuker of them all. Hosea 5:2

Chapter 6

A Spiral Staircase of Fire

And a fire was kindled in their company; the flame burned up the wicked. Psalm 106:18

That day in September of 1979 marked the beginning of a downward spiral that is very hard to describe. Since I never talked about it, I didn't ever try to describe it.

If I had been on a quest for love in all the wrong places before, it took on a whole new embodiment now. The first and only person I confessed my abortion to very soon after became my first husband. He accepted me and did not judge me. For that, I was grateful enough to pledge my life to him, and that was the foundation of my first marriage. He was ten years older than me, married to another woman at the time, and they had two very small children together. He divorced her and married me, and I became an instant stepmom. Every time I saw their little faces, I was reminded of the baby I would never get to see.

Inside, a part of me had died. It was not a conscious death; it was a death I kept buried deep, deep inside.

This stronghold, along with many others that grew, kept me in private bondage for most of my adult life.

On the surface, you would never know. I dove headfirst into being "perfect" in every way. I had to be the "perfect" wife, at least for a while. I had to be the "perfect" stepmom, the "perfect" mom. Oh, and I can't forget the "perfect" career woman. The only way I could keep the pain buried within me was to cover it with perfect success.

I refused to think about what I had done; I refused to mourn my baby. I refused to acknowledge the embryo had been my baby. I never talked about it. After my first confession to the first man I would marry, we never spoke of it again. Though I did not choose to numb my pain with drugs or alcohol, I certainly can totally understand why many women choose that path.

With every passing day, I walked farther and farther away from the God who loved me, who had never left me, who was so ready to forgive me, who still lived deep inside of me and longed for our ONEness, even after the horrible thing I had done.

1 John 4: **15**Whosoever shall confess that Jesus is the Son of God, God dwelleth in him, and he in God. **16**And we have known and believed the love that God hath to us. God is love; and he that dwelleth in love dwelleth in God, and God in him. **17**Herein is our love made perfect, that we may have boldness in the day of judgment: because as he is, so are we in this world. **18**There is no fear in love; but perfect love casteth out fear: because fear hath torment. He that feareth is not made perfect in love.

Chapter 7

Why

During the years, I made several attempts to come back to God. Once again, I believed so many lies of the enemy. I truly, truly believed God was mad at me; I believed He hated me. Yes, I know God hated what I had done, but I turned that hatred away from what I had done, and I internalized it and believed God hated me. Therefore, I strongly hated myself.

Every time I would enter a church, the overwhelming emotions would surface, and I would cry. I could never explain my tears to myself, let alone to anyone else, so I would just stop going to church. I believed that even if I continued to go to church, they would kick me out if they ever found out what I had done. For a few years, I stopped seeking God altogether.

From the first day of my life, I have a very clear, very conscious memory of a love for babies. I have always loved babies, and babies love me. I was the last person anyone would ever think would have an abortion, especially me. Every time I hold a baby, I am reminded of the baby I have in heaven, the one I killed. For many years, that remained a constant torment in my life, even though I buried the torment, kept it hidden and, at times, hidden it from even myself. I doubt, however, that anyone was ever born believing they would ever have an abortion; but God knew . . .

I raised two exceptional stepsons, and I gave physical birth to two other exceptional sons. My stepsons were dark-haired and beautiful, and my birth sons were beautiful and blond. So every time I looked at them, I always wondered what my daughter in heaven would have looked like. I was sure she would be blond. I was blond, and her father was blond. I had straight hair but her father's was naturally curly, so I always picture her with blond curls. I know she is beautiful. I have often wondered if my torment would have been less had I not born other children. Today, I know it probably would have been worse. I also lived with the fear I would not be able to have children because of my sin.

Ten years out from the abortion, I found myself married, raising four children and starting a brand-new career; I was driven. At the time, I just thought I was born competitive and ambitious. Perhaps I was, but today I see the drive as a force to cover what I wanted to keep hidden; a force to show the world I wasn't such an awful woman; a force to prove to God I was worth loving; a force to overcome my past. This drive was my inability to face what I had done.

For others, they find their past as a roadblock to any success in life. They can't be happy because they don't feel they deserve happiness. They can't succeed because they don't feel they deserve success. They can't love because they will be giving to them what they couldn't give to "it", the baby they refuse to acknowledge as a baby.

Twenty years out, and I find my life in shambles; I am living the life of a lie. My marriage is failing, my kids are hurting, and the spiral staircase of fire has lead me smack dab into the middle of hell. You see, we can only live a lie for a while before reality hits us right in the face.

Each of us who have aborted a baby finds various ways to anesthetize our pain. For some, it's drugs, alcohol and/or sex, and for others, it's a hellish-driven ambition, material possessions, prescription medications, multiple marriages, etc.. Not one of us escapes. If someone had told me how that one act would affect the rest of my life, would I have gone through with it? For me, if one person had told me that was a living baby on the inside of me, I never could have done it. If I had seen one picture from a sonogram or an ultrasound, it never would have happened, but that is me. It's not about me; never has been, never will be.

God tells us over and over again, in His Word, He will never leave us and never forsake us. I had believed the lie that God had left me, that He was mad at me and hated me. God's Word is full of the truth that He was right there with me in that room, holding me, loving me, as I acquiesced to an abortion of my baby girl. In fact, I now know that Jesus, himself, lifted my baby girl from my womb and carried her into the arms of her Heavenly Father; she lives there now, waiting on her earthly mother.

There are hundreds of reasons why women have abortions: to save their own life; to keep from hurting a loved one; because she doesn't have the means to support a new baby; because she doesn't know how to care for a baby (or another one); because she doesn't know the father; because she was raped; because it doesn't matter if she has an abortion; because she doesn't deserve to be a mother; because the baby has a deformity or disease (or at least that's what the doctor said) or because she doesn't know what else to do, etc., etc.

Each of us has a unique experience before, during and after the abortion; there are no two stories identical in abortion. There is a numbness after we get the news of the pregnancy, there is a numbness as we walk through the abortion and a numbness we live in after the abortion. We own our own experience, our own fear, our own pain, our own guilt, our own condemnation, our own downward spiral. We don't want anyone to compare theirs to ours, nor should we. God made each of us unique and one-of-a-kind. Our experience of abortion is just as one-of-a-kind, and yet there are many things we share in common. Each of you reading this book that has had an abortion recognize yourself in many of the lines, and yet it's not quite your story.

Some of us have had abortions before we've had any other children. Many of us have had abortions after we already have had other children. Some of us have abortions in our teens, while others are much older. There are some of the details that are the same, and others that are completely different.

There are some absolutes that have never changed and will never change.

Jesus Christ, the same yesterday, and today, and forever. Hebrews 13:8

Chapter 8

Now I can SEE

Before I formed you in the womb, I knew you.
Jeremiah 1:5

God hates murder; therefore, He hates abortion. Abortion is murder of a living baby. There are several places in the Bible God refers to the unborn as babies or babes. You can read the story of Jacob and Esau where God called the unborn babes. John the Baptist was unborn when, as a baby, he leapt in his mother's womb when Mary approached Elizabeth.

Scripture condemns the shedding of innocent blood (Deuteronomy 19:10; Proverbs 6:17; Isaiah 1:15; Jeremiah 22:17). While the killing of all innocent human beings is detestable, the Bible regards the killing of children as particularly heinous (Leviticus 18:21; 20:1-5; Deuteronomy 12:31). The prophets of Israel were outraged at the sacrifice of children by some of the Jews. They warned that it would result in the devastating judgment of God on their society (Jeremiah 7:30-34; Ezekiel 16:20-21, 36-38; 20:31; compare 2 Kings 21:2-6 and Jeremiah 15:3-4 together).

According as he hath chosen us in him before the foundation of the world, that we should be holy and without blame before him in love. Ephesians 1:4

Time does not exist with God. In Psalm 90:4, Moses used a simple, yet profound, analogy in describing the timelessness of God: "For a thousand years in Your sight are like a day that has just gone by, or like a watch in the night." The eternity of God is contrasted with the temporality of man. Our lives are but short and frail, but God does not weaken or fail with the passage of time.

In a sense, the marking of time is irrelevant to God, because He transcends it. Peter, in 2 Peter 3:8, cautioned his readers not to let this one critical fact escape their notice—that God's perspective on time is far different from mankind's (Psalm 102:12, 24-27). The Lord does not count time as we do; He is above and outside of the sphere of time. God sees all of eternity's past and eternity's future. The time that passes on earth is of no consequence from God's timeless perspective. A second is no different from an eon; a billion years pass like seconds to the eternal God.

God thought of me and you before he formed the earth.

Father, I will that they also, whom thou hast given me, be with me where I am; that they may behold my glory, which thou hast given me: for thou lovedst me before the foundation of the world. John 17:24

He did not look down on that dark, gloomy day in 1979 and say, "Oh my goodness, Elizabeth, I never knew you would abort the baby girl I gave you." Oh,

He knew I would, and He loved me anyway. In fact, He sent Jesus for me in spite of my sin.

The Bible reassures me in 2 Samuel, and again in Matthew, that my baby girl is indeed in heaven. King David stated he would see his baby in heaven. Jesus told his disciples there is a special place in heaven for babies.

God called me at an early age; I always felt His pull. God is sovereign; He calls us to die to self so we can rise in Him. It's not about us; never has been, never will be. He knew I would walk in the valley of the shadow of death, and He always knew I would come back to Him. He used every bad circumstance in my life, He used every bad decision I ever made, to take me to the end of myself so I could submit to Him and truly belong to Him. He allowed me the freedom to fail, because in my weakness, He is made strong. When I am spent, He is glorified.

Chapter 9

Hope

"He will wipe away every tear from their eyes; there shall be no more death; nor sorrow, nor crying. There shall be no more pain." Revelation 21:4

It took me a very, very long time to come to these truths: to know that God never stopped loving me; to believe God always knew I would have that abortion, and yet He still chose me; to know that He took all my sins, including the abortion, and threw them as far as the east is from the west; that God remembers my sins no more.

My journey to this day was a day-by-day renewing of my mind, a change from my thoughts being of the world to my thoughts being the thoughts of Christ. I had to sort through the lies I had believed. I had to recognize the strongholds and demons attached to my soul that kept me from moving forward for a long time, and that kept me stuck in my hell.

I wish I could tell you an instantaneous miracle took place, and I guess from one perspective, it did. I was on a fiery path of destruction; I felt my life was over. I was divorced, my children were hurting and my world was turned upside down. Everything I ever believed in was destroyed.

Three years after my divorce, I find myself still searching for love in all the wrong places. I had not made one step towards the God who was always waiting for me. Still in the pit, a friend introduced me to a wonderful man, a stable man, a kind man, a caring man, a strong man, a man who prayed one prayer every night before he slept; "God, please send me a woman to love. You know I have a lot of love to give." He had been single for almost ten years, and he had given up hope of ever finding the right one.

He never asked me about my past then, and he never asks me about my past now. To him, the past is the past, and that's where it belongs. When I need to talk about the past, he is my steady shoulder. He never judges me; he accepts me just as I am. He is an angel sent to me by a loving God, because he had the faith to pray a simple prayer every night.

Not everyone will have the kind of love and acceptance from their husband as I have been blessed with. Not every woman who has aborted will ever be able to tell her husband, or her children; nor should she. The decision to talk is a very personal decision. God will guide you on when to talk and with whom to talk with.

To hide it inside is to allow the poison to kill you; but to talk to the wrong person is to speak death over them, and perhaps over your relationship. If God has placed a burning need inside of you to confess to someone after you have made your confession to God, go to your Pastor's wife. Find a professional Christian counselor. Be very, very careful to whom you confess your abortion. If it hurts the other person, is that really the person you are to confess to?

Bottom line, I had to realize God chose me, and I made a decision to choose God, no matter what – I did NOT give up. This I say to you now: "Never, ever give up." God is real. God is in you. God longs for you to become ONE with Him.

Jesus was with you when you aborted your baby. Jesus was with your baby when you aborted him/her. Jesus allowed us to make our decisions, to set our own course, and suffer our own consequences. God is sovereign.

God never changes; God was God when I was innocent and pure; God was God when I was sexually promiscuous; God was God before I aborted, and God was God when I aborted and God is God even after I aborted.

God gave me a second chance in my second marriage. He sent me a man who would take me to church, who would sit and allow me to cry every time I went to church, and never ask me why. He allowed me to seek God on my own timing and in my own way. He never invaded my privacy, but he never turned me away when I needed him. He is everything I ever dreamed a husband would be and far, far more.

God gave me this man, my second husband, as His gift. God knew he would be my second husband before I ever turned back to God. That's the miracle, and that is proof solid of God's love for me in the depths of my sin. God had a good plan for me before the foundations of the earth were laid, and that plan included my second chance at love. God's grace was for me before I even knew what it was. God is the God of a thousand second chances and more. It is never too late with God.

God's grace is free; I can't earn it, and neither can you. I cannot earn God's forgiveness for my sins, but I can accept His free grace freely given to me, while

I was yet a sinner, through the blood of His precious, only begotten son. His baby; God's baby; Jesus, and so can you.

Jesus willingly died for my sins. He could have called ten thousand angels and stopped it all, but He didn't. He took the rejection; He took the shame; He took the beatings, the name-calling, the crucifixion, and He died for ME. He died for the baby I killed.

God knew I had to come to the end of myself before I would ever submit to Him. God allowed me to wallow in my sin and torment to my very weakest moment so He could be made strong.

God never lies; He always tells the truth. God loves me, and God loves my baby in heaven. God doesn't remember my sin, neither should I. God's grace is sufficient, and His mercies are new every morning.

There were days when I would scream to God (yes, He can handle all of our emotions; after all, He created them and gave them to us), and ask Him how many times He would forgive me of the same sin. He lovingly pointed me to Matthew 18:21, where Jesus tells the disciples to forgive each other seventy times seven in a day.

God is faithful. When I am not faithful, God never moves; He never changes. My first decision: go to church. My second decision: keep going to church (even though it was the hardest thing to do at that time in my life). My third decision: One day, I decided to pray. I don't know what I said, but now I know God loves to hear our voice, no matter what's said. My fourth decision: To ask God to forgive me (yes, I did ask a thousand times because of my unbelief, not because I had to . . . He forgave me the very first time I asked). My fifth decision: To start the process of forgiving myself. Eventually, I started a daily intimate time with

God where I read His word, I prayed and I listened for His voice. This intimate time with God is the core to who I am today (in Christ) and my total restoration.

Along the way, God gave me Jeremiah 29:11, and He personalized it into something like this: "For I know the plans I have for you, Elizabeth, plans to prosper you and not to harm you, to give you a future and a hope." If I had a nickel for every time I prayed that scripture over myself, I would be a very wealthy woman. This one scripture guided me for several years, until I determined not to give up and to get into God's word; He gave me many, many scriptures to guide me, heal me and restore me. In hindsight, I know this is the very reason I have the Godly husband I have today.

Ask God to forgive you; totally and completely submit to Him (this is a daily process that will never end this side of heaven); find a loving church home, find a safe person to help you (I left this step out, and I stayed stuck far too long); be faithful to God through your church attendance (yes, it is a vital step; not because we "have" to, but because we want to; because we love Him); pray unceasingly (okay, start with a few words a day, and build up to conversations with God); listen for His voice; read His word and don't give up (not necessarily in this order).

God cares that you hurt. He collects every tear you cry and keeps them in His bottle, and He writes down every one of them you shed in His book. He feels your pain. God sent His only son to the cross to give you life to the full and overflowing. He wants you to have hope; He wants you to live in hope.

God never fails; His way is the only way. He is right on time, every time. You can live heaven on earth now, the torment can stop, and you can help others climb out of their hellhole. There is always hope.

Chapter 10

The Reason I Write . . .

Romans 8:28 "And we know that all things work together for good to them that love God, to them who are the called according to his purpose."

I never ever ever thought I would write a book. I certainly never thought it would be about my abortion. I didn't even really want to write a book, and certainly not about abortion.

But more than I want air to breath, I want to please my Father. And my Father is all about the hurting . . . and He created me before the foundations of the earth to help the hurting . . . and if I can help just one person, one woman, one girl, if I can save the life of just one baby . . . then every tear I cried, every horrible pain I felt, every tragedy I endured will be worth it all.

God saved me and He saved me for a purpose. He didn't save me just so I can live a restored, whole life. Yes, He restored me completely. Yes, my life is now whole. I can stand in front of a hurting woman and hold her while she cries and tells me about her abortion and I can walk away whole. My life is not my own. My life belongs to my Heavenly Father. In my heart, I believe

God will use my pain to help someone get through theirs. I believe God will use this book to save an unborn baby. God will use this book to heal a women's broken heart. For Him, I write. For you, I expose my deepest darkest secrets.

Dueteronomy 28 tells me of the blessings that will overtake me if I hear His voice and obey. So I am writing this book. No, I do not have to write the book for God to love me. I don't have to do a single solitary thing ever again in my life, and God will still love me beyond my wildest imagination. But He created me for a purpose. Part of that purpose is this book.

I am not responsible for the results of this book. I am responsible to God for writing this book. I am responsible for writing and speaking the truth. My story is not over until eternity. And your story is far from over.

My baby is not dead, she is very much alive and living in the Kingdom of Heaven with her Father God. I will see her again. I will love what I see. She would not come back, even if given the chance. Where she lives is so much beyond anything I could ever offer her here on earth. No, she would never ever come back. She is happy. She never cries, she never hurts. She will never have her heart broken, she will never suffer physical or emotional pain.

This prayer states very succinctly why I write this book:

Father God,

Thank you for you, thank you for your Son who died to save me and to save the precious woman reading this book. Father, I thank you that through this book, the woman reading this book is SEEING you and she is feeling you alive in her heart and she is realizing that you and she are ONE and you love her beyond her wildest imagination.

I thank you Father that my little baby girl is alive and well and she lives with you in the mansion you created just for her in heaven. I thank you she has never felt pain, never had a broken heart, and never feels the effects of the sins of her mother. Thank you Father that my little girl runs, she laughs, she plays, and with her very spirit she loves you, Father God, and she loves me.

Thank you Father for placing this book in this woman's hands right this second in time. Thank you for allowing this book to draw her closer to you. Thank you for placing angels of mercy in her path so she can talk out her pain to someone safe. Thank you for giving her hope and a future of fullness and happiness and completeness in you.

In Jesus I pray.

Amen

I could choose to live in regret. I could choose to live condemned. I could choose to live in guilt and shame. But instead, I choose to accept the free gift God offered me for such sins as mine: His total and complete forgiveness and redemption. As Paul told King Agrippa in Acts 26: "I think myself happy." If I don't choose happiness, then I am telling Jesus His death was in vain, it wasn't good enough to ensure my happiness. I have a choice. And I choose life.

The reason I write.

Jeremiah 30:1-2
The word, which came to Jeremiah from the Lord saying, thus saith the Lord God of Israel WRITE all the words, which I have spoken to you in a book.

Proverbs 24:10
If you are slack in the day of distress your strength is limited.

Proverbs 24:11-12 11 Rescue those who are unjustly sentenced to die; save them as they stagger to their death. 12 Don't excuse yourself by saying, "Look, we didn't know." For God understands all hearts, and he sees you. He who guards your soul knows you knew. He will repay all people, as their actions deserve.

Proverbs 24:11
Deliver those who are being taken away to slaughter and those who are staggering to slaughter oh hold them back.

Psalm 102:18
This shall be written for the generation to come: and the people who shall be created shall praise the Lord.

Psalm 40:16 let all those that seek thee rejoice and be glad in thee; let such as love thy salvation say continually, the Lord be magnified.

Psalm 40:17 But I am poor and needy; yet the Lord thinketh upon me; thou art my help and my deliverer; make no tarrying, O My God.

Isaiah 6:6-8 . . . with a burning coal he had taken from the altar with a pair of tongs He touched my lips with it and said "See, this coal has touched your lips. Now your guilt is removed, and your sins are forgiven." Then I heard the Lord asking, "whom should I send as a messenger to this people? Who will go for us?" I said, "Here I am Lord, Send Me."

Through my journey, God asked me to SEE things as He SEES things. Only when I allowed myself to SEE me as God SEEs me was I able to forgive myself. The stronghold melted off with the new vision of God.

SEE:

Exodus 14:13 . . . Fear ye not, stand still, and see the salvation of the LORD, which he will shew to you to day.

2 Kings 6:17 And Elisha prayed, and said, LORD, I pray thee, open his eyes, that he may SEE. And the LORD opened his eyes . . .

Job 19:26 . . . yet in my flesh shall I see God:.

Psalm 27:13 I had fainted, unless I had believed to SEE the goodness of the LORD in the land of the living.

Acts 26:18 To open their eyes (SEE), and to turn them from darkness to light, and from the power of Satan unto God, that they may receive forgiveness of sins, and inheritance among them which are sanctified by faith that is in me.

Once I asked God to allow me to SEE as He SEE's, He showed me in great detail that He and I are ONE. It started with scriptures of God telling Jesus he was sent to earth so we could be ONE as He and his Father are ONE. With the revelation of our ONENESS, I suddenly understood how Jesus could feel everything I feel. I had heard so many times that when we hurt He hurts. I heard that he felt every pain we could ever feel. How could that be? Jesus was a man, I am a woman. He had never given birth. He had never killed his baby. Until I understood my ONENESS with Him I had no answers to so many of my questions.

He does feel what we feel. He cries every tear we cry. His Spirit and our Spirit are ONE.

ONE:

John 17:11 And now I am no more in the world, but these are in the world, and I come to thee. Holy Father, keep through thine own name those whom thou hast given me, that they may be one, as we are.

1 John 4:4 Ye are of God, little children, and have overcome them: because greater is he that is in you, than he that is in the world.

1 John 4: 7Beloved, let us love one another: for love is of God; and every one that loveth is born of God, and knoweth God. 8He that loveth not knoweth not God; for God is love.

1 John 4:12 If we love one another, God dwelleth in us, and his love is perfected in us

As a woman reading this book, you may be thinking about having an abortion. You may be a woman who has had an abortion. You may be the mother or grandmother of a young woman who is pregnant and lost without answers of what to do. You may have a friend in this situation. You may not know what to say, who to turn to, what to do and you are reading my book. I want to give you the first step: pray to your Father in heaven who loves you beyond infinity right now, right where you are, without you changing one single solitary thing, He loves you. He longs to hear your voice. He knows every thought you have ever had in your head and He knows every thought before you ever think it. There is nothing hidden from Him. Pray to Him like this:

Father God,

You know who I am, you know what I am. You know everthing about me and everything about my circumstances. There is nothing hidden from you. You already know I am hurting so bad.

God I don't know what to do. I don't know how to do it. I don't know my next step. Please, God, show me. Make yourself real to me. I am humbling myself in my weakness, asking you to make me strong.

God, somehow, someway, get me through this. Let me know you are with me, that I am not alone. Send me the right person to help me, to speak truth to me. Give me the right prayers to pray with the desire to speak to you every day. Show me scriptures to guide me, Lord.

God, your Word says if I seek, I will find. I am seeking you now Lord, like I never have before. Please let me find you and your way. Help me no longer to make this about me, but to make all of my life about you.

Today, I pledge to trust you God. Today, I pledge to seek you in all my decisions. Today, I choose to believe you have heard my prayer and you are answering my prayer. I thank you Father God for loving me even when I am not lovable. I thank you for hearing my cries, capturing my tears, and guiding my steps.

In Jesus I pray,

Amen

CPSIA information can be obtained at www.ICGtesting.com
Printed in the USA
LVOW05s0948230314

378431LV00004B/7/P

9 781629 522449